The alphabet joined the circus.
Find and circle each letter.

ABCDEFGHIJKLMNOPQRSTUVWXYZ

1

A

was an **ant**

Who seldom stood still

Who made a nice house

In the side of a hill.

Trace **A**. Then write **A**.

Write **A** by the two pictures that begin like 🍎.

B

was a **bat**
With an arm in a sling;
He flew 'round in circles
With only one wing.

Trace B. Then write B.

Write B by the two pictures that begin like .

C

was a **camel**

Whose hump was misplaced;

When it was found

He fixed it with paste.

Trace C. Then write C.

Write C by the two pictures that

begin like .

D was a **dancer**

Who danced all day long;

When doing a two-step

She'd burst into song.

Trace **D**. Then write **D**.

Write **D** by the two pictures that begin like .

E was an **egg**

Our feisty hen laid;

When she was done

She asked to be paid.

Trace **E**. Then write **E**.

Write **E** by the two pictures that

begin like ⬯.

F was a **fox**
Who was clever and sly;
He crept in the kitchen
To eat cherry pie.

Trace **F**. Then write **F**.

Write **F** by the two pictures that begin like .

G

was a **gander**

With fuzzy white down;

He dressed like a man

When he went into town.

Trace G. Then write G.

Write G by the two pictures that begin like .

H was a **heron**

Who stood in a stream;

The length of his neck

And his legs was extreme.

Trace **H**. Then write **H**.

Write **H** by the two pictures that begin like  .

I was an **itch**

That bothered a bear;

He scratched and he scratched

Till he lost all his hair.

Trace I. Then write I.

Write I by the two pictures that begin like .

J was a **jogger**

Who tried not to stop;

Around and around

He went in one spot.

Trace **J**. Then write **J**.

Write **J** by the two pictures that begin like 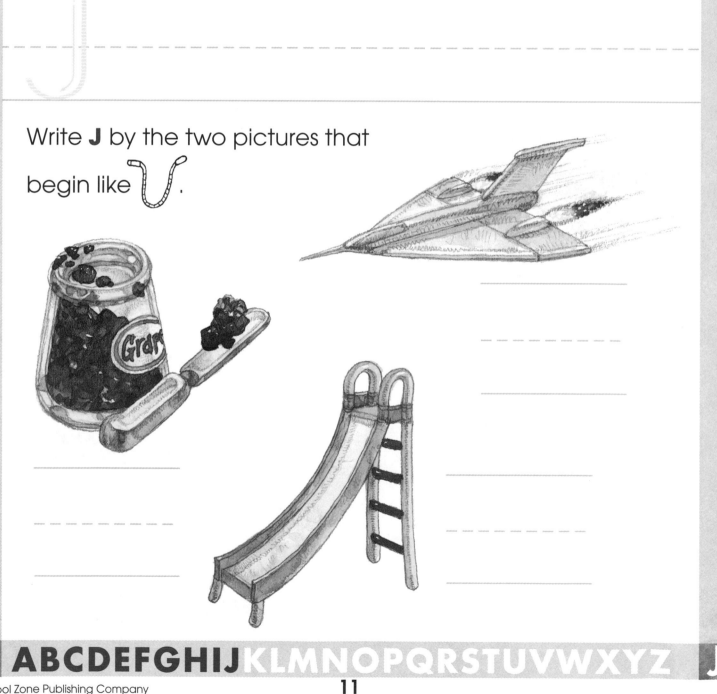.

K

was a **kitten**

Who lived on a farm;

She saw her black shadow,

Then ran to the barn.

Trace **K**. Then write **K**.

Write **K** by the two pictures that begin like .

was a **llama**

Who had his own house;

He rented two rooms

To a frog and a mouse.

Trace L. Then write L.

Write L by the two pictures that begin like .

M was a **mouse**
Who was digging a hole;
He was looking for diamonds
But found only coal.

Trace **M**. Then write **M**.

Write **M** by the two pictures that

begin like 🌙.

14

N

N was a **narwhal**

Whose tooth did not gleam;

He went to the dentist

Who polished it clean.

Trace **N**. Then write **N**.

Write **N** by the two pictures that begin like .

O

was an **otter**,

His wife was a loon;

They ate all their dinners

By the light of the moon.

Trace **O**. Then write **O**.

Write **O** by the two pictures that begin like  .

© School Zone Publishing Compa

P

was a **parrot**

Who talked all day long;

But she couldn't say "Polly,"

She got it all wrong.

parachute
perimeter
parliament
peninsula
popcorn
planet
primate
pumpkin
AWK!

Trace **P**. Then write **P**.

Write **P** by the two pictures that begin like .

Q was the **Queen**

Who couldn't stand bugs;

She trapped them in vases

And baskets and mugs.

Trace **Q**. Then write **Q**.

Write **Q** by the two pictures that begin like ❓.

Q ABCDEFGHIJKLMNOPQRSTUVWXYZ Q

R was a **raven**
Who lived in a tree;
He sat on a branch
And watched the TV.

Trace **R**. Then write **R**.

Write **R** by the two pictures that begin like .

S was a **stork**

With a very long bill,

Who swallowed down fishes

And frogs to his fill.

Trace S. Then write S.

Write S by the two pictures that begin like ⭐.

T

was a **toad**

Who forgot how to hop;

He took hopping lessons

And now he can't stop.

Trace **T**. Then write **T**.

Write **T** by the two pictures that

begin like .

U

was my **uncle**
Who never sat down;
He slept standing up
In a flannel nightgown.

Trace **U**. Then write **U**.

Write **U** by the two pictures that begin like .

© School Zone Publishing Compar

V was a **violet**
In love with a rose;
When they went out to dinner
She wore her best clothes.

Trace **V**. Then write **V**.

Write **V** by the two pictures that begin like .

W

was a **worm**

Who ate mud and dirt;

He chomped on a rock

That made his jaw hurt.

Trace **W**. Then write **W**.

Write **W** by the two pictures that begin like

X

X marks the spot

On an old treasure map;

If you don't find the gold,

You'll fall in a trap.

Trace **X**. Then write **X**.

Write **X** by the *one* picture that

begins like .

Y

was a **yak**
From the land of Tibet;
Lonesome for home,
He took off in a jet.

Trace **Y**. Then write **Y**.

Write **Y** by the two pictures that begin like .

Z was a **zebra**

Who bought many socks;

He carried them home

In a large yellow box.

Trace **Z**. Then write **Z**.

Write **Z** by the two pictures that begin like 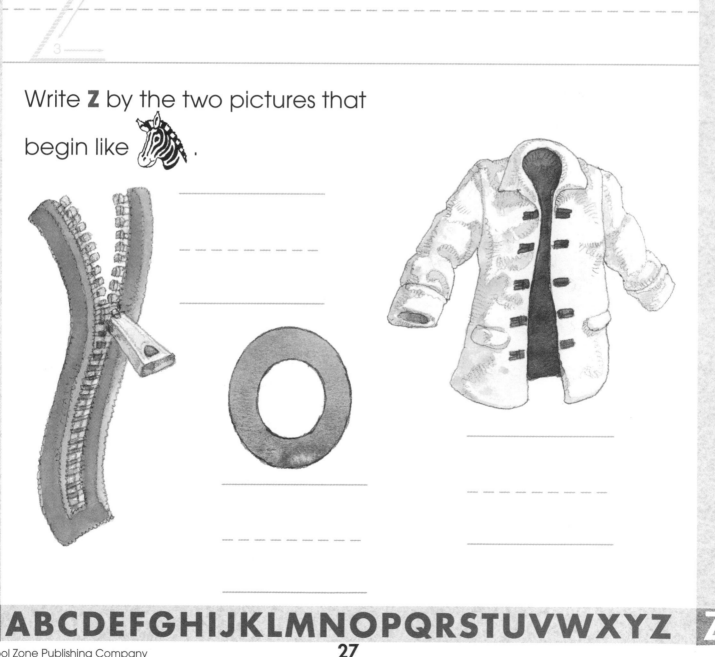.

A
B
C
D
E
F
G

Follow the path. Write the beginning letter for each picture word.

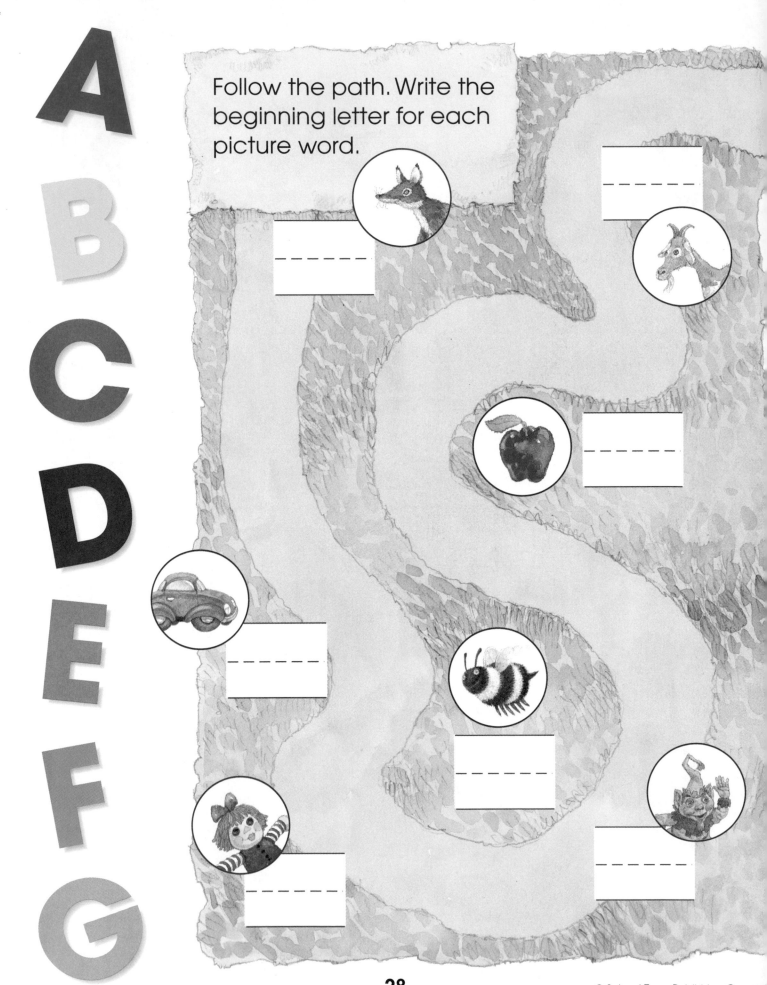

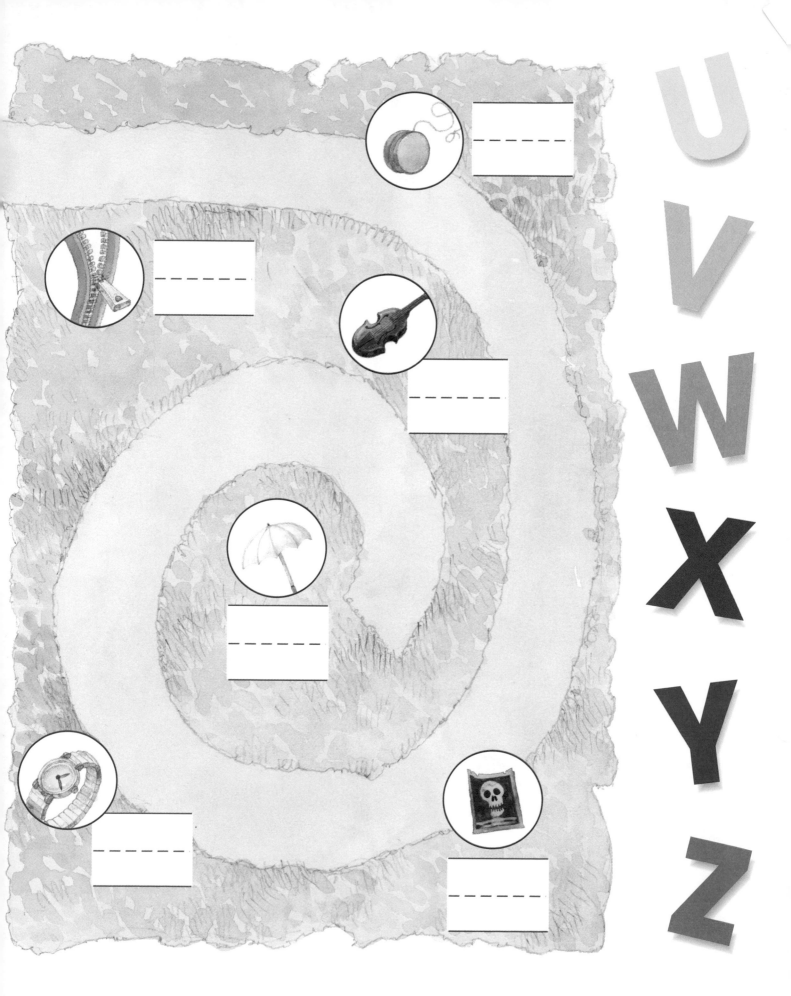

Draw a line from each picture to the matching letter.

A B C D E F G H I J K L M N O P Q R S T U V W X Y Z

Find and circle each letter.

a b c d e f g h i j k l m n o p q r s t u v w x y z

was an **apple**
That fell from a tree;
A worm that was in it
Waved to me.

Trace **a**. Then write **a**.

Write **a** to begin each word.
Draw a line from the picture to the picture word.

_____ pple

_____ pron

_____ ngel

b

was a **bee**

Who flew upside down;

When he would smile

It looked like a frown.

Trace **b**. Then write **b**.

Write **b** to begin two words. Write **b** to end a word.
Draw a line from the picture to the picture word.

_____ all

_____ utterfly

we _____

C

was a **cat**

Who went out every night;

He didn't come home

Until dawn's early light.

Trace c. Then write c.

Write c to begin each word.
Draw a line from the picture to the picture word.

ake

ow

arrot

© School Zone Publishing Compa

d was a **dog**;

In the morning, he howled;

He woke up a bear

Who grumbled and growled.

Trace **d**. Then write **d**.

Write **d** to begin two words. Write **d** to end a word.
Draw a line from the picture to.the picture word.

_____ **og**

_____ **inosaur**

bir _____

was an **elephant**

With really big feet;

The animals scattered

As he walked down the street.

Trace **e**. Then write **e**.

Write **e** to begin each word.
Draw a line from the picture to the picture word.

lephant

gg

nvelope

f

was a **fish**
Who felt he was sick;
He knitted a sweater
That was cozy and thick.

Trace **f**. Then write **f**.

Write **f** to begin two words. Write **f** to end a word.
Draw a line from the picture to the picture word.

_____ ish

_____ ox

el _____

g was a **goat**

With two curly horns;

He's been full of mischief

Since the day he was born.

Trace **g**. Then write **g**.

g²

Write **g** to begin two words. Write **g** to end a word.
Draw a line from the picture to the picture word.

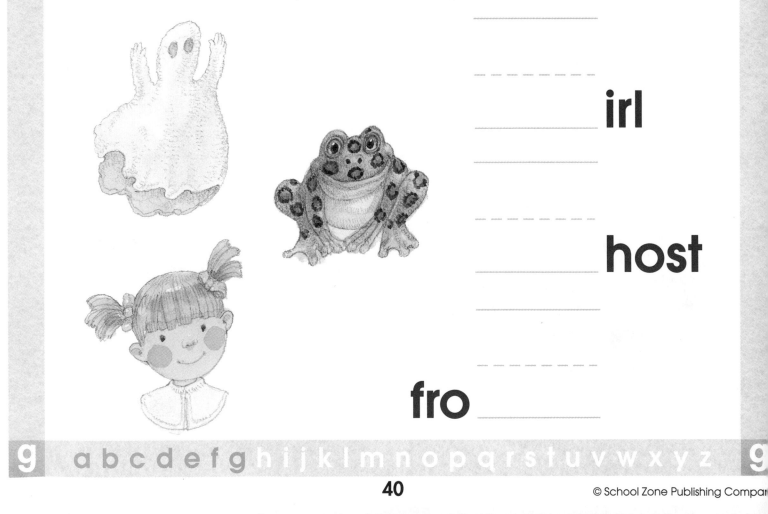

_____ irl

_____ host

fro _____

h

was a **hat**
So tall and so green;
Birds nested in it
And couldn't be seen.

Trace **h**. Then write **h**.

Write **h** to begin each word.
Draw a line from the picture to the picture word.

_____ **en**

_____ **eart**

_____ **orse**

i was an **inchworm**

Who measured all day;

When evening arrived,

It was his time to play.

Trace i. Then write i.

Write i to begin each word.
Draw a line from the picture to the picture word.

_____ **nk**

_____ **nsect**

_____ **gloo**

j was a **juggler**

Throwing balls in the air,
And when he would miss
They would land in his hair.

Trace **j**. Then write **j**.

Write **j** to begin each word.
Draw a line from the picture
to the picture word.

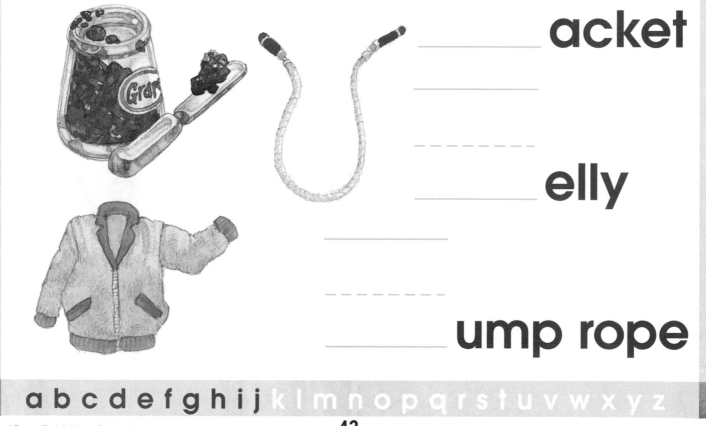

_____ acket

_____ elly

_____ ump rope

k

k was a **koala**
Who wanted to fly;
He made wings out of leaves
And flew in the sky.

Trace **k**. Then write **k**.

k

Write **k** to begin two words. Write **k** to end a word.
Draw a line from the picture to the picture word.

_____ **itten**

_____ **ey**

duc _____

was a **lion**,

While asleep he would snore;

The sound shook the walls

Of his neighbor next door.

Trace I. Then write I.

Write I to begin two words. Write I to end a word.
Draw a line from the picture to the picture word.

_____ **ake**

_____ **eaves**

bel _____

m

was **Miss Molly**

Who turned in her toes

And hung down her head

Till her knees touched her nose.

Trace **m**. Then write **m**.

m

Write **m** to begin two words. Write **m** to end a word.
Draw a line from the picture to the picture word.

_____ ittens

_____ oney

dru _____

n

was a **newt**

Who bought a new boat,

So he could go skiing

With his friend the white goat.

Trace **n**. Then write **n**.

Write **n** to begin two words. Write **n** to end a word.
Draw a line from the picture to the picture word.

_____ et

_____ uts

clow _____

School Zone Publishing Company

O was an **owl**

Who kept saying "Whooo!"

He met a fine cow

Who answered with "Moo!"

Trace o. Then write o.

Write o to begin each word.
Draw a line from the picture to the picture word.

_____ live

_____ wl

_____ x

p was a **pig**

With a curly pink tail;

He ordered a straightener

That came in the mail.

Trace **p**. Then write **p**.

Write **p** to begin two words. Write **p** to end a word.
Draw a line from the picture to the picture word.

_____ **ear**

_____ **uppy**

cu _____

 was a **quail**

Who lived in a tree;

She made tiny cookies

When friends came to tea.

Trace q. Then write q.

Write q to begin each word.
Draw a line from the picture to the picture word.

_____ **uilt**

_____ **ueen**

_____ **uarter**

r

was a **rabbit**

With fur soft and white;

He escaped from his hutch

And hopped out of sight.

Trace r. Then write r.

Write r to begin two words. Write r to end a word.
Draw a line from the picture to the picture word.

ake

ose

sta _____

s was a **snowman**

With an orange carrot nose;

Although it was cold,

He never wore clothes.

Trace s. Then write s.

Write s to begin two words. Write s to end a word.
Draw a line from the picture to the picture word.

_____ un

_____ ocks

boot _____

t was a **tortoise**
With a shell red and black;
Friends played checkers
On top of her back.

Trace **t**. Then write **t**.

Write **t** to begin two words. Write **t** to end a word.
Draw a line from the picture to the picture word.

_____ urtle

_____ urkey

ca _____

u was an **umbrella**

That turned upside down;

It filled up with rain

And ducks swam around.

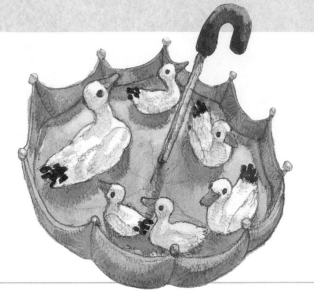

Trace **u**. Then write **u**.

Write **u** to begin each word.
Draw a line from the picture to the picture word.

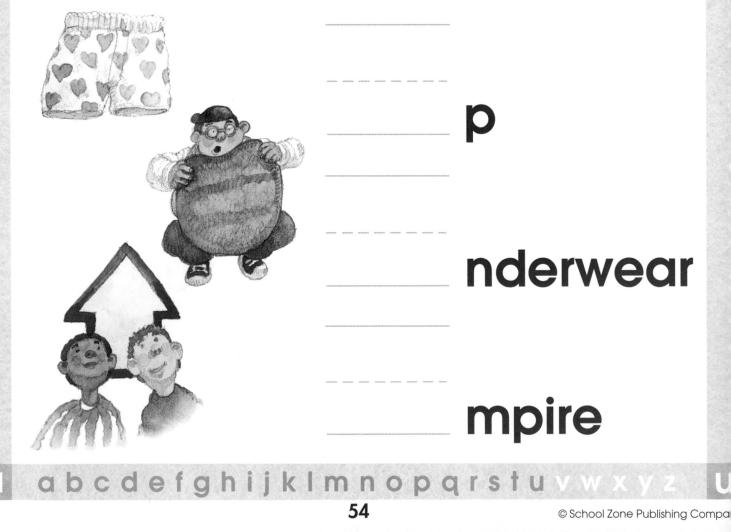

_____ **p**

_____ **nderwear**

_____ **mpire**

V was a **violin**

That had a bad squeak;

It gave you a headache

That lasted a week.

Trace **v**. Then write **v**.

Write **v** to begin each word.
Draw a line from the picture to the picture word.

_____ an

_____ ase

_____ olcano

W

was a **whale**
Who sailed for the stars,
Refueled, and ate lunch
At the diner on Mars.

Trace **w**. Then write **w**.

w w

Write **w** to begin two words. Write **w** to end a word.
Draw a line from the picture to the picture word.

_____ agon

_____ olf

co _____

© School Zone Publishing Compa

X

was an **x-ray**
With film black and white;
It showed things inside me
That were not in my sight.

Trace **x**. Then write **x**.

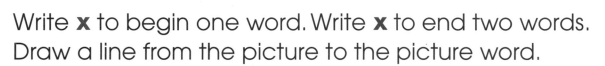

Write **x** to begin one word. Write **x** to end two words.
Draw a line from the picture to the picture word.

_____ -ray

bo _____

fo _____

a b c d e f g h i j k l m n o p q r s t u v w x y z

y

y was a **yo-yo**

That rolled on the floor;

The string wasn't broken,

It was out to explore.

Trace **y**. Then write **y**.

Write **y** to begin two words. Write **y** to end a word.
Draw a line from the picture to the picture word.

_____ o-yo

_____ arn

ha _____

Z was a **zeppelin**

That flew through the sky

While its crew of three monkeys

Ate hot apple pie.

Trace **z**. Then write **z**.

Write **z** to begin each word.
Draw a line from the picture to the picture word.

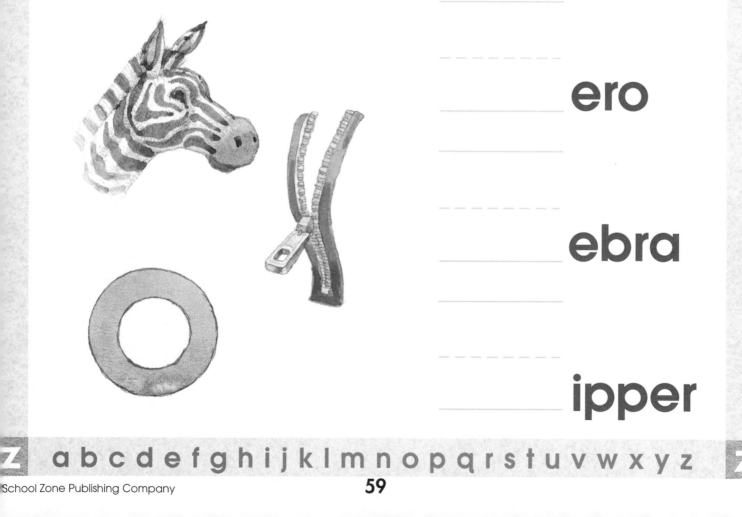

_____ ero

_____ ebra

_____ ipper

It's rush hour for the alphabet! The first letter of each animal's name should match the letter it is driving.

Find the drivers who are driving the wrong letter, and mark them with an **X**.

beep! beep!

HEY WATCHit buddy!!

Write the letter that begins each word.

62

Whenever you see animals gathered like this, they're trying to say something! Write the first letter of each picture name.

a b c d e f g h i j k l m n o p q r s t u v w x y z

Circle the numbers 1-9 hidden in this picture.

I
one

One mouse is in the house.

Trace **I**. Then write **I**.

Trace **one**. Then write **one**.

one

Circle everything that there is only **one** of below.

2
two

Two dogs are chasing frogs.

Trace 2. Then write 2.

2

Trace two. Then write two.

two

Circle the groups of two.

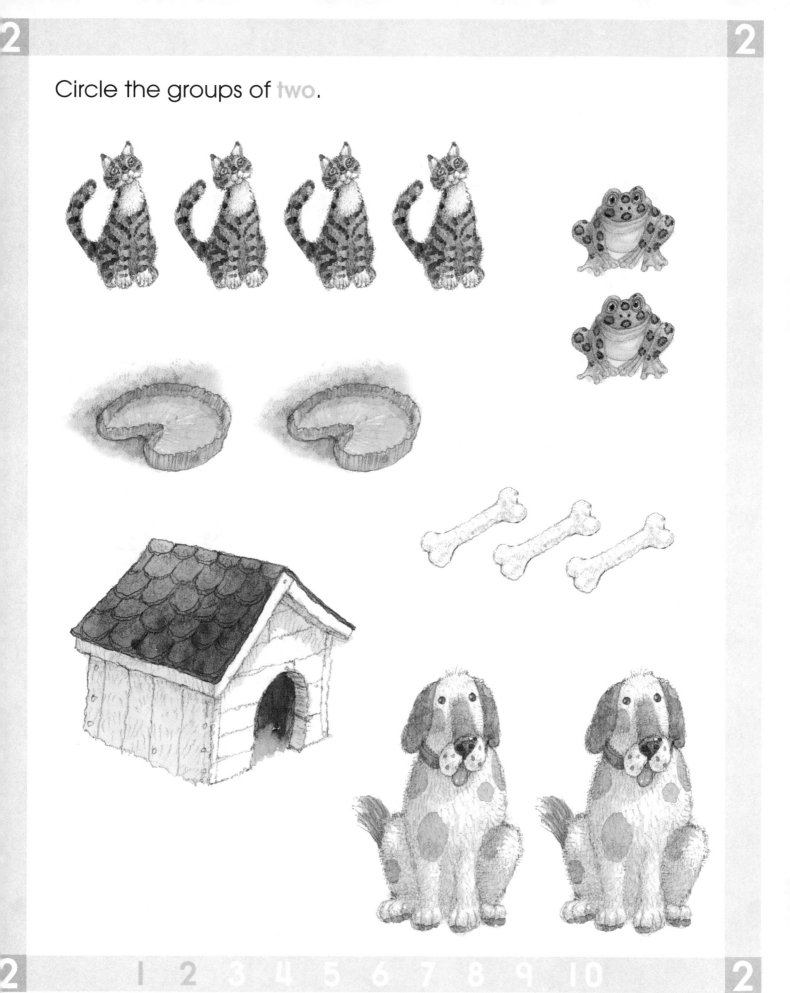

1 2 3 4 5 6 7 8 9 10

3
three

Three cats are wearing hats.

Trace **3**. Then write **3**.

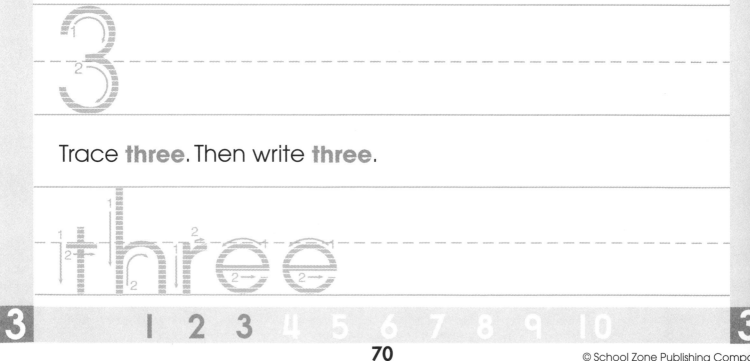

Trace **three**. Then write **three**.

Circle the groups of **three**.

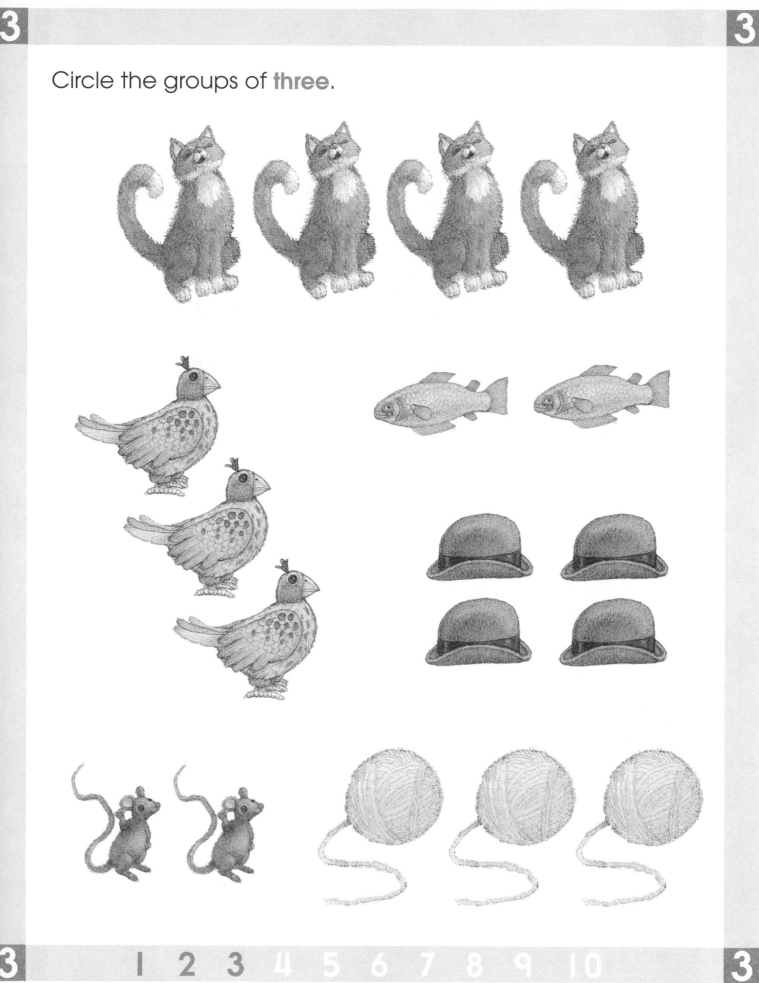

4
four

Four goats are rowing boats.

Trace 4. Then write 4.

Trace **four**. Then write **four**.

Circle the groups of **four**.

5
five

Five pigs are wearing wigs.

Trace **5**. Then write **5**.

Trace **five**. Then write **five**.

Circle the groups of **five**.

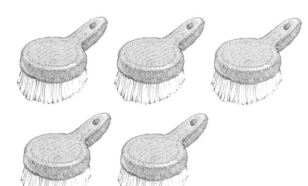
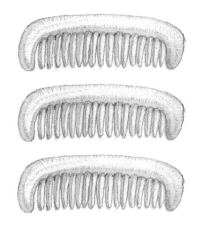

School Zone Publishing Company

6
six

Six chicks are doing tricks.

Trace **6**. Then write **6**.

6

Trace **six**. Then write **six**.

six

Circle the groups of **six**.

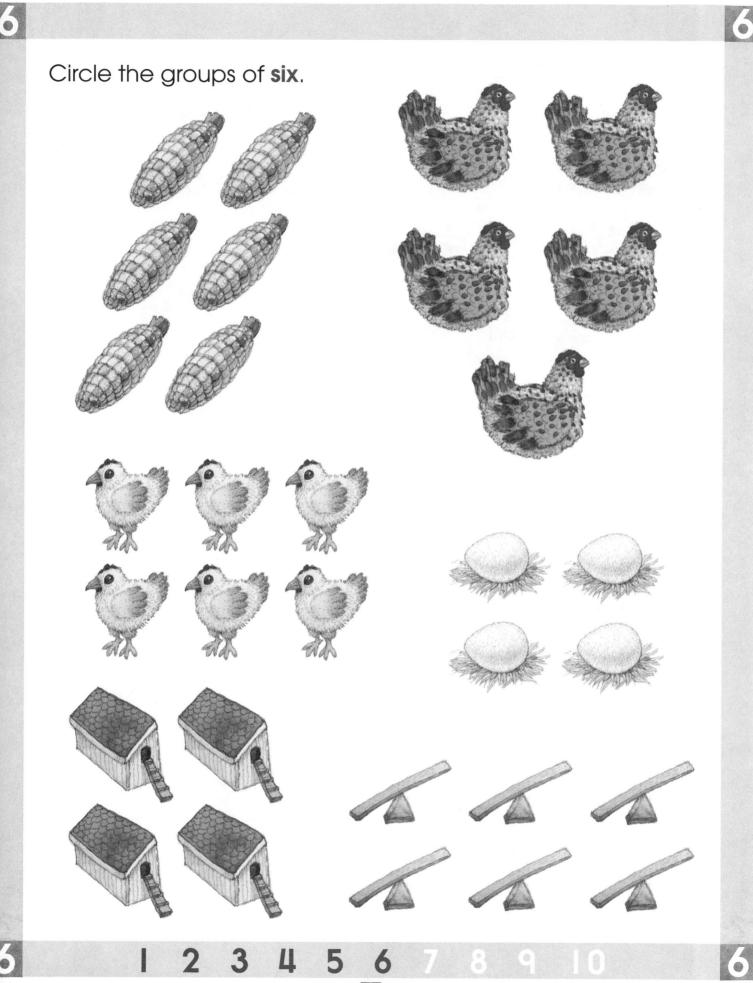

School Zone Publishing Company

7
seven

Seven sheep are in a jeep.

Trace 7. Then write 7.

Trace **seven**. Then write **seven**.

seven

1 2 3 4 5 6 7 8 9 10

Circle the groups of **seven**.

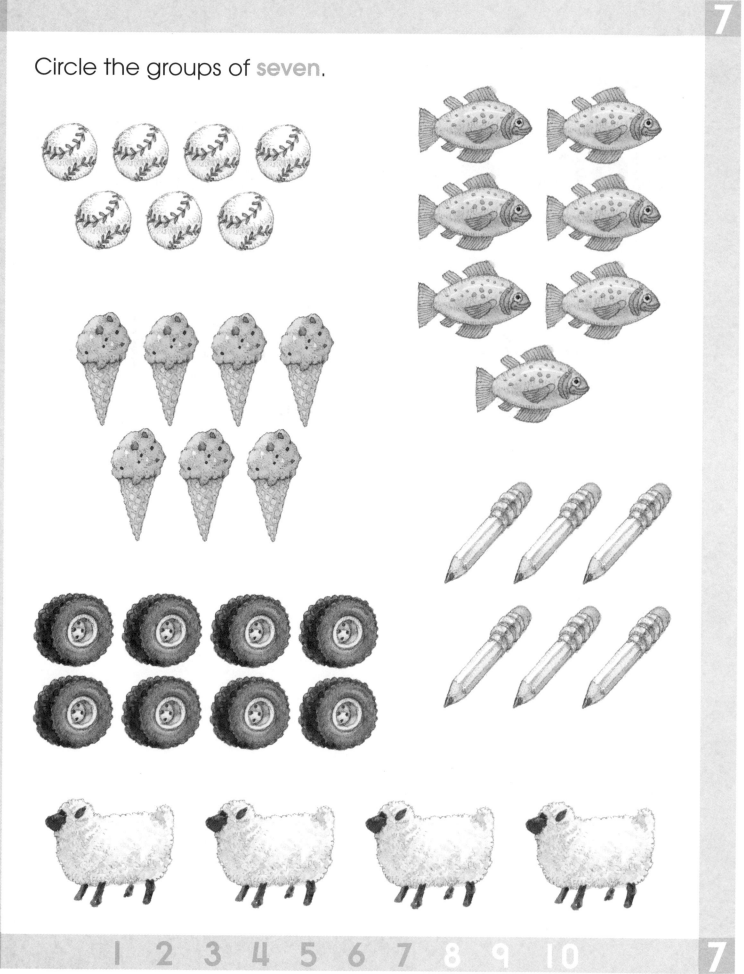

8
eight

Eight ants are wearing pants.

Trace 8. Then write 8.

Trace **eight**. Then write **eight**.

Circle the groups of **eight**.

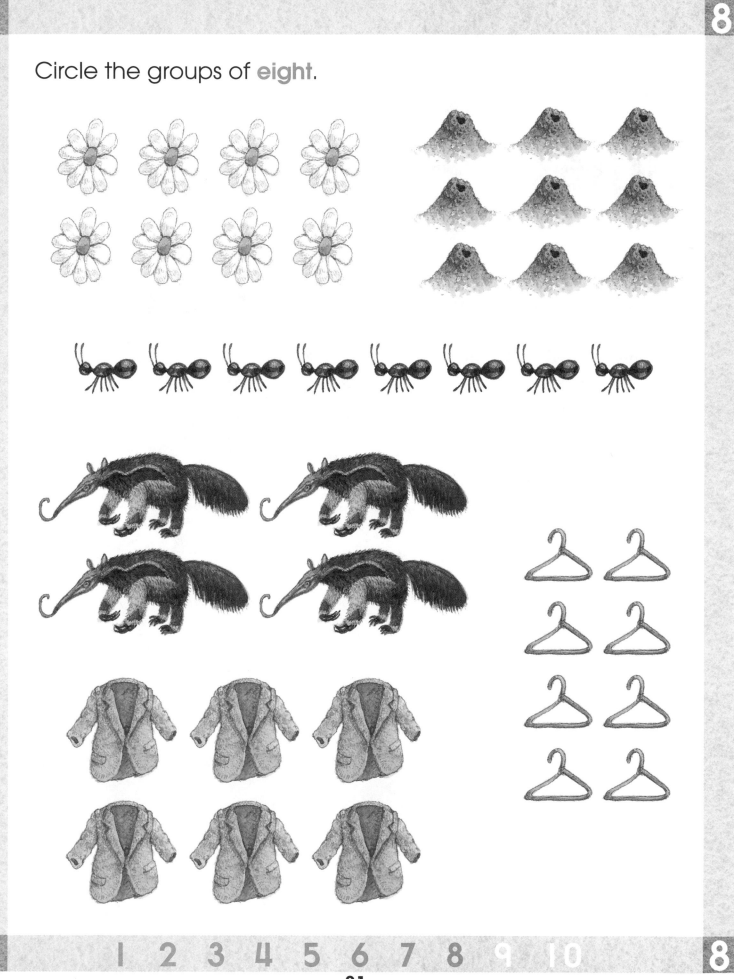

9
nine

Nine fish are in a dish.

Trace 9. Then write 9.

Trace nine. Then write nine.

© School Zone Publishing Compan

Circle the groups of nine.

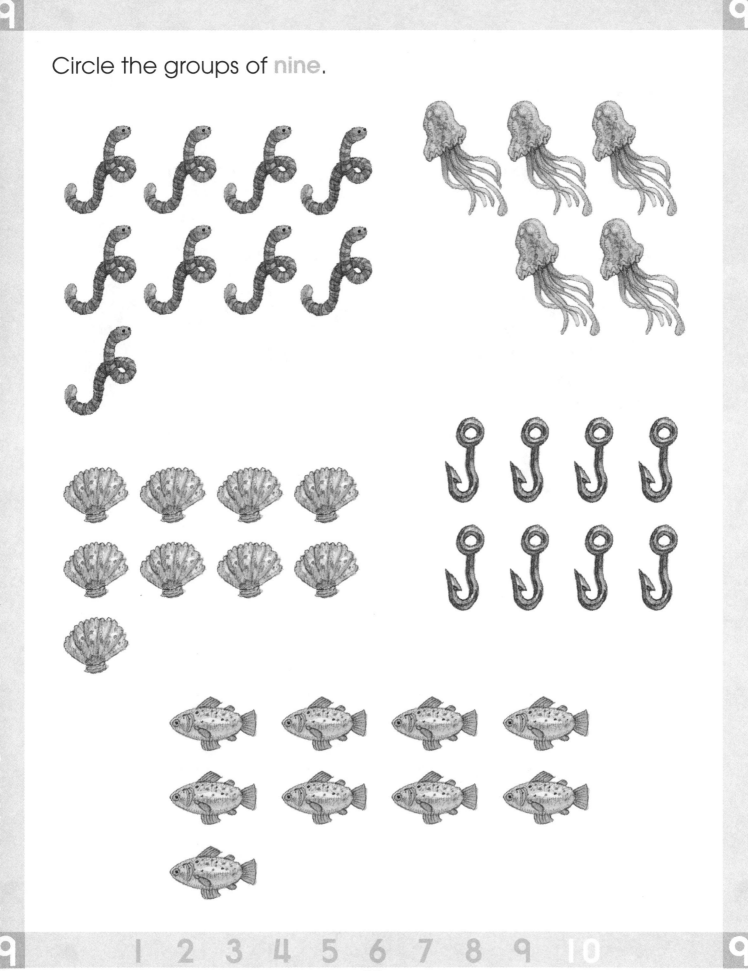

10
ten

Ten bees are having tea.

Trace 10. Then write 10.

Trace **ten**. Then write **ten**.

Circle the groups of ten.

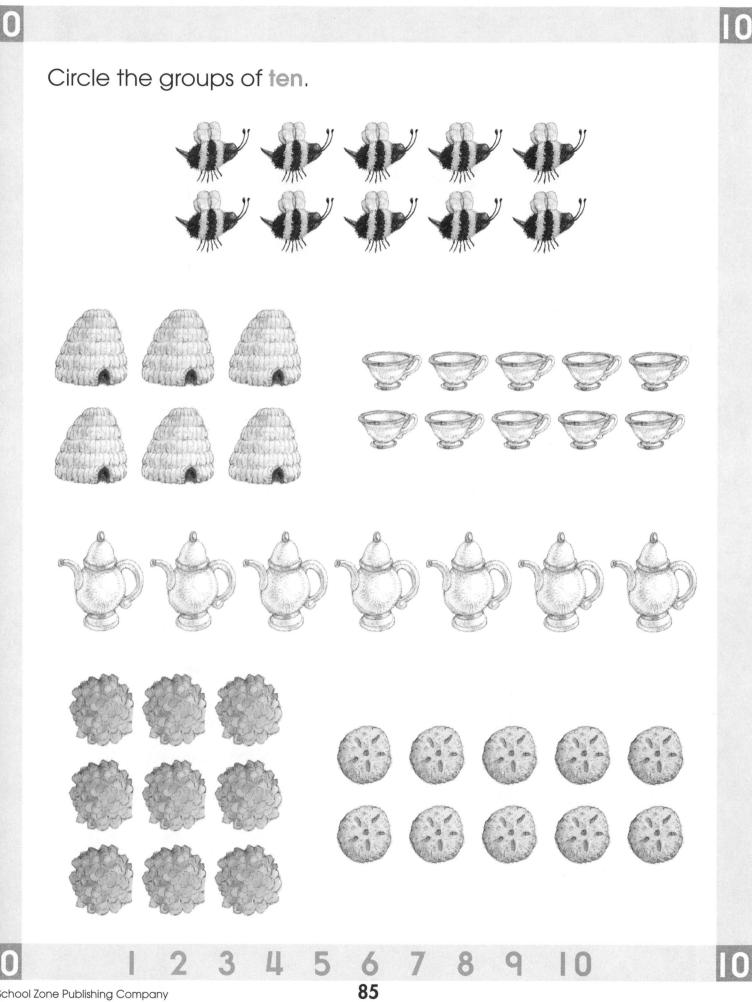

Count the objects. Then circle the correct number.

8 7 10

4 3 5

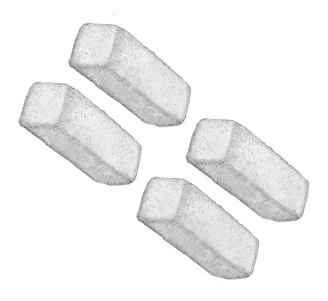

4 5 7

7 8 9

Count the objects. Then circle the correct number.

5 6 7

8 9 10

6 7 8

2 3 4

What number comes next?
Write the missing numbers.

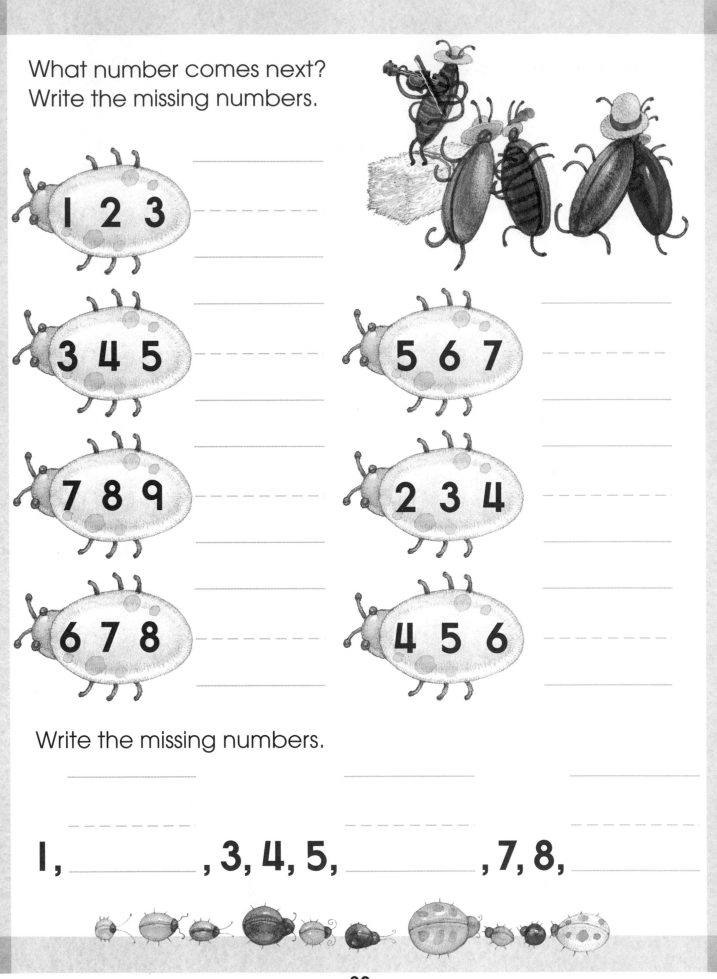

1 2 3 _____

3 4 5 _____

5 6 7 _____

7 8 9 _____

2 3 4 _____

6 7 8 _____

4 5 6 _____

Write the missing numbers.

_____   _____

_____   _____

1, _____, 3, 4, 5, _____, 7, 8,

What number comes before?
Write the missing numbers.

_____ 4 5 6

_____ 5 6 7

_____ 7 8 9

_____ 6 7 8

_____ 8 9 10

_____ 2 3 4

_____ 3 4 5

Continue the pattern.

6, 7, 8, 6, 7, 8, 6, _____ , _____

Write the number below each group.
Circle the number that is greater.

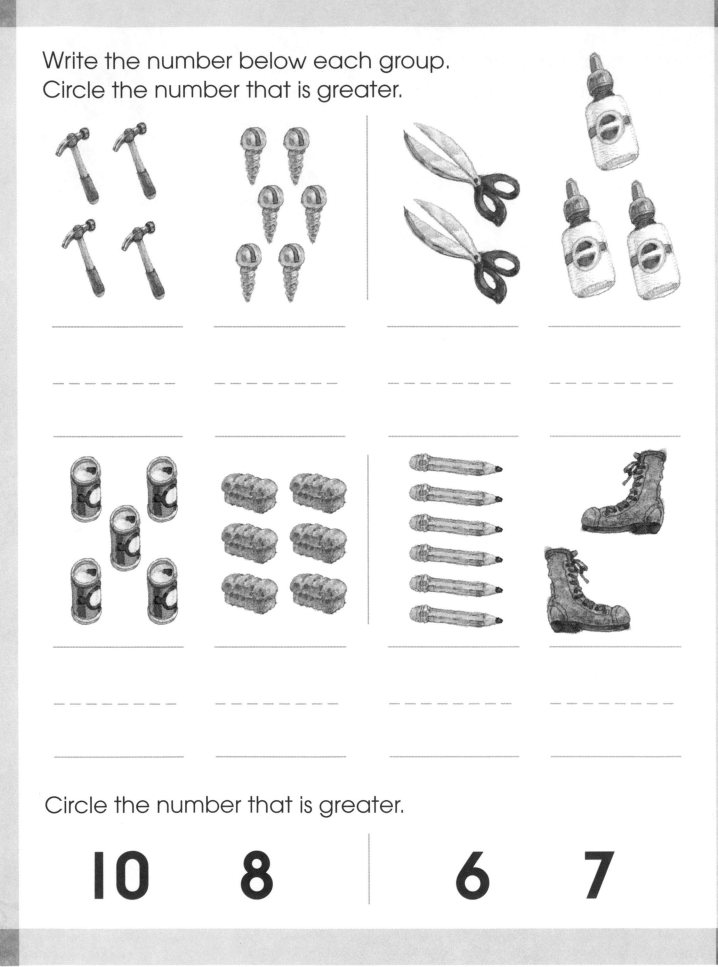

Circle the number that is greater.

10   8   6   7

Write the number below each group.
Circle the number that is less.

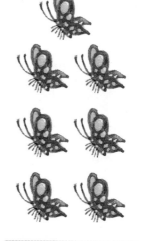

_____

- - - - - - - - - - - -

_____

Circle the number that is less.

5 7 9 8

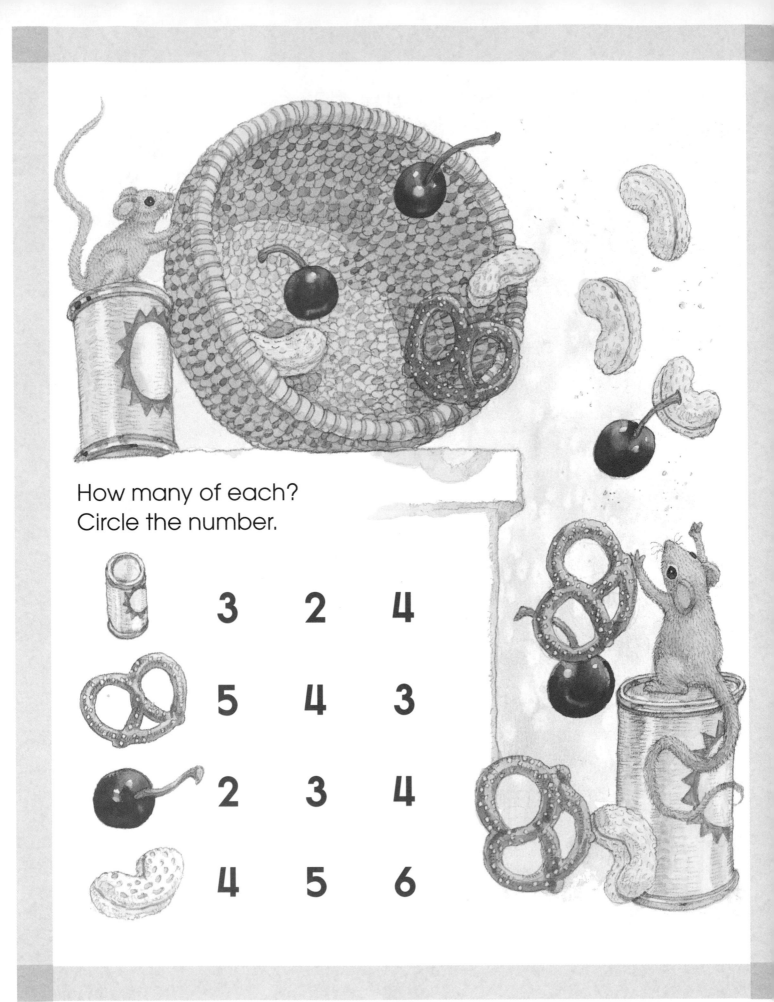

How many of each?
Circle the number.

3   2   4

5   4   3

2   3   4

4   5   6

How many of each thing?
Guess. Then count.

	🌼	🍴	🥛
Guess			
How Many?			

Match the Numbers

Draw a line from each number to the correct group.

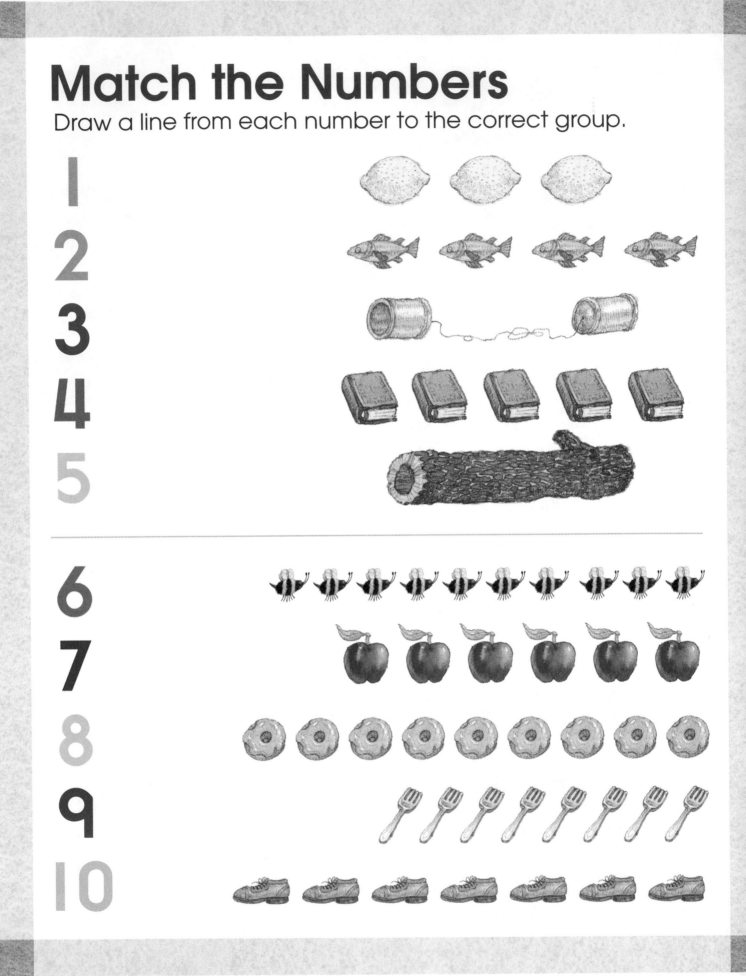

1
2
3
4
5

6
7
8
9
10

Circle the picture that shows the **opposite** of the first picture.

big

full

hot

in

Greater Than

Greater means more than.

4 is greater than 3.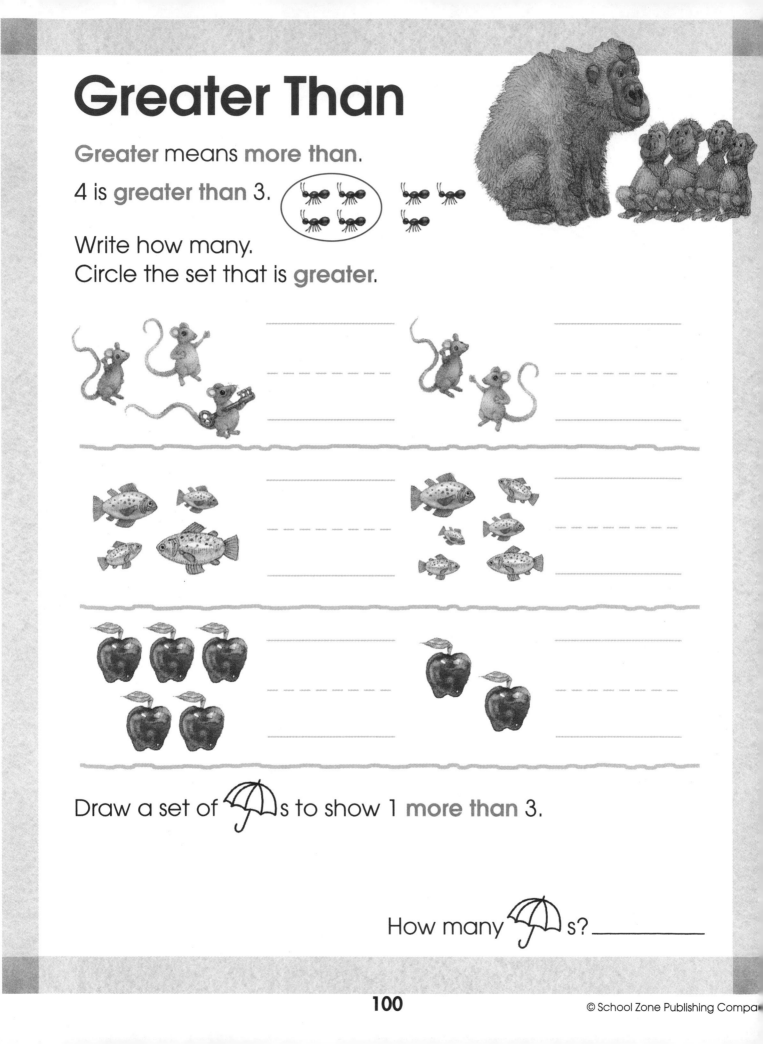

Write how many.
Circle the set that is greater.

Draw a set of ⛱s to show 1 more than 3.

How many ⛱s? _____

Less Than

Less means **not as many**.

2 is **less than** 3.

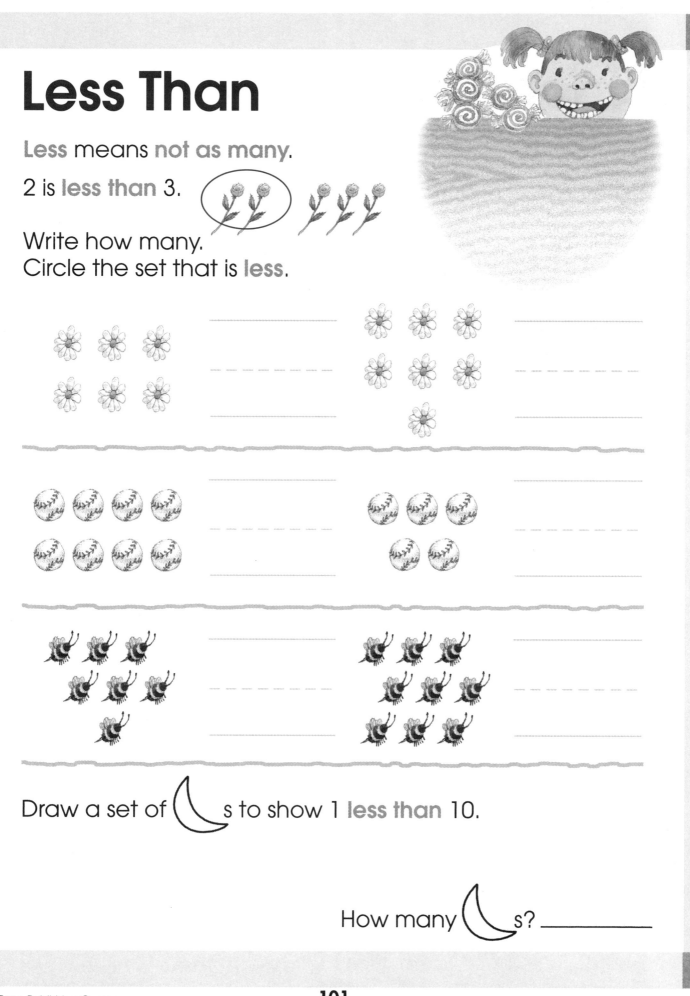

Write how many.
Circle the set that is **less**.

Draw a set of 🌙 s to show 1 **less than** 10.

How many 🌙 s? _____

Bigger

This  is **big**. This is **bigger**.

Circle the picture that is **bigger** than the first picture.

Smaller

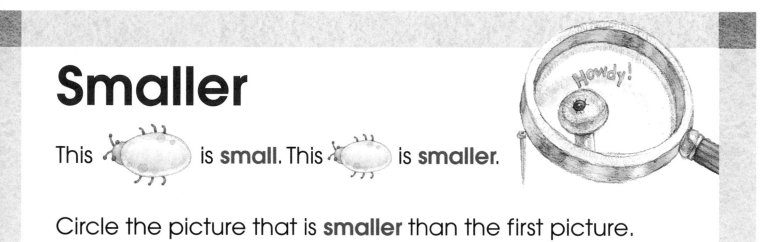

This is **small**. This is **smaller**.

Circle the picture that is **smaller** than the first picture.

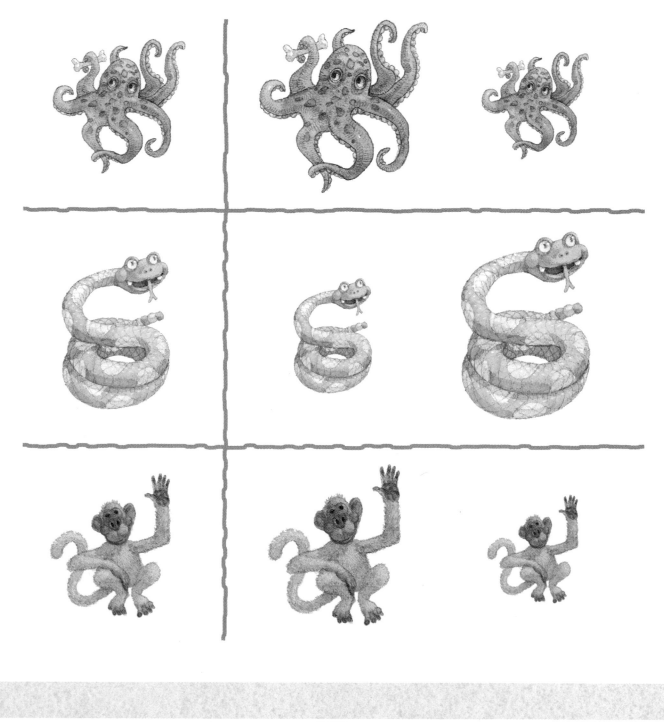

Same Size

These 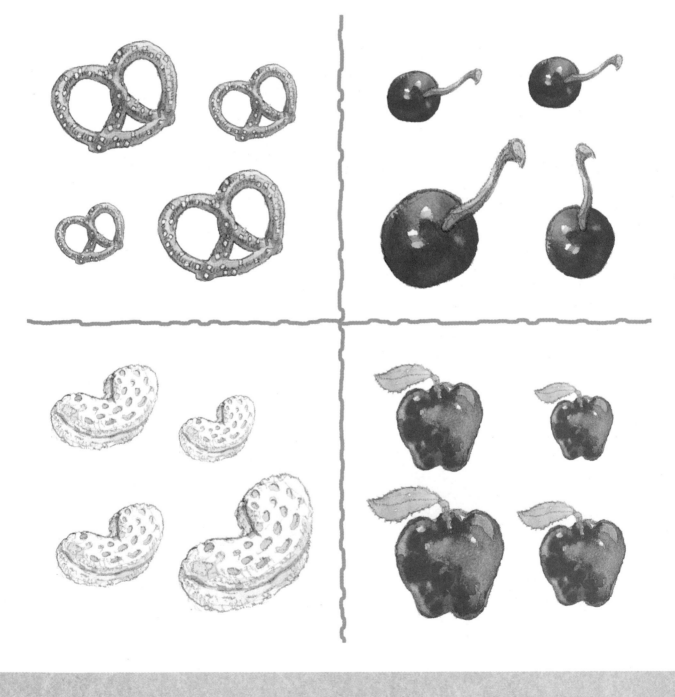 are the **same size**.

Circle two pictures that are the **same size**.

Make a Pair

A 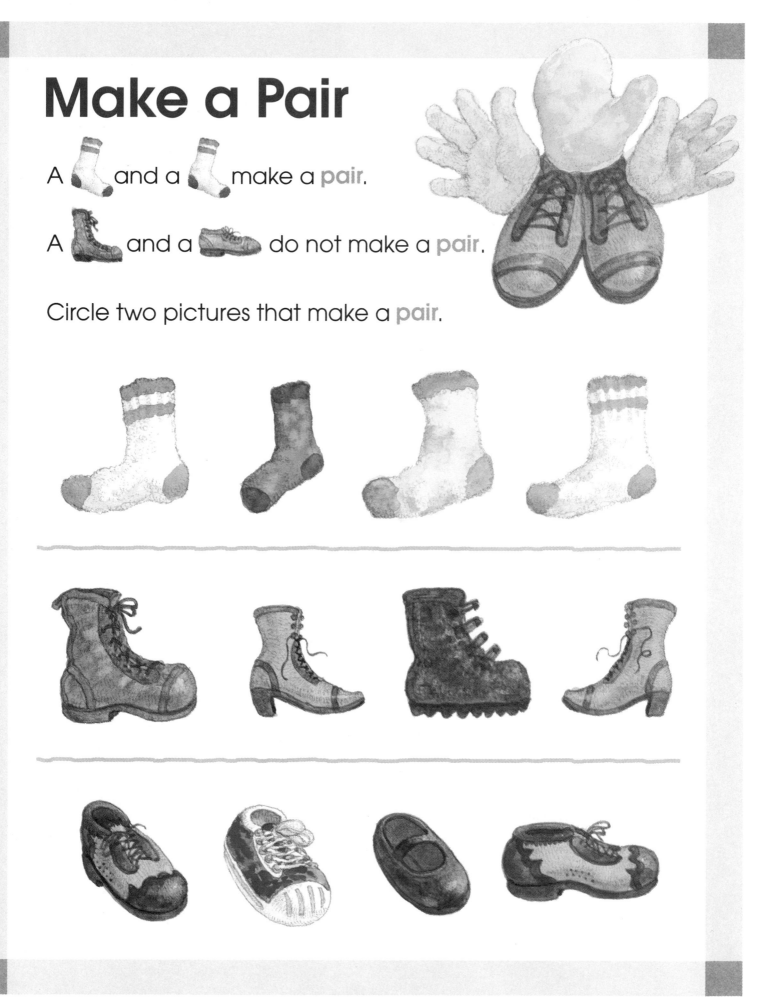 and a make a **pair**.

A and a do not make a **pair**.

Circle two pictures that make a **pair**.

Top/Bottom

The tomato is on top.
The lettuce is on the bottom.

Circle the  that is on top.

Circle the that is on the bottom.

Left/Right

This  is on the **left**.

These are on the **right**.

Circle the picture that shows the same as the first picture.

Left

Right

Rhyming

 **rhymes** with .

Say the name of each picture.
Circle two that **rhyme** in each group.

Circle two that **rhyme** in each group.

What Goes Together?

 and  go together.

Circle the picture that **goes** with the first one.

Hello, Rover residence...

Circle the picture that **goes** with the first one.

chool Zone Publishing Company

Maze

Help the ship get to the dock.

Circle

This is a **circle**. ●

Color two circles blue.

How many s can you find? _____

Square

This is a **square**.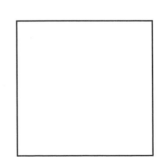

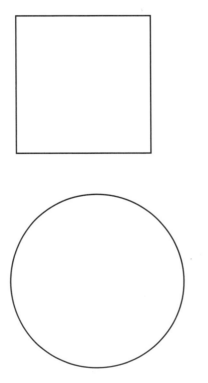

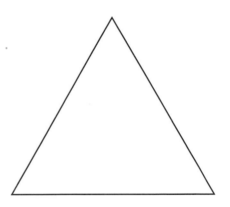

Color two squares **red**.

116

How many ⬜s can you find? _____

Rectangle

This is a **rectangle**. ▮

Color two rectangles orange.

How many ☐s can you find?

Triangle

This is a **triangle**.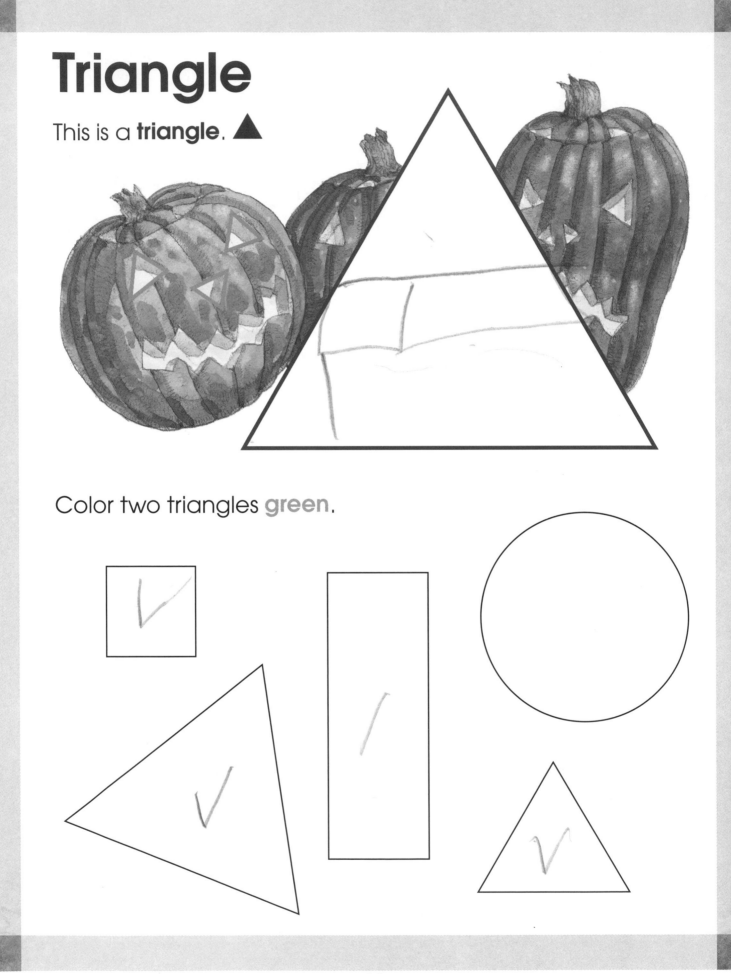

Color two triangles green.

How many s can you find? _____

121

Same

These are the **same**.

Circle two that are the **same** in each group.

122

Circle the picture that is the **same size** as the first one.

Different

These  are the **same**. This is **different**.

Circle the picture that is **different**.

Circle the picture that is **different**.

First, Next, Last

Write 1 by what happened first.
Write 2 by what happened next.
Write 3 by what happened last.

First, Next, Last

Write **1** by what happened **first**.
Write **2** by what happened **next**.
Write **3** by what happened **last**.

First, Next, Last

Write **1** by what happened **first**.
Write **2** by what happened **next**.
Write **3** by what happened **last**.

Whimsy Readiness Basics, Grades K-1 024